VICTORIAN LIFE

VICTORIAN CLOTHES

LYN GASH

Wayland

VICTORIAN LIFE

A VICTORIAN CHRISTMAS

A VICTORIAN FACTORY

A VICTORIAN HOLIDAY

A VICTORIAN SCHOOL

A VICTORIAN STREET

A VICTORIAN SUNDAY

VICTORIAN CLOTHES

VICTORIAN TRANSPORT

HOW WE LEARN ABOUT THE VICTORIANS

Queen Victoria reigned from 1837 to 1901, a time when Britain went through enormous social and industrial changes. We can learn about the Victorians in various ways. We can still see many of their buildings standing today, we can look at their documents, maps and artefacts – many of which can be found in museums. Photography, invented during Victoria's reign, gives us a good picture of life in Victorian Britain. In this book you will see what Victorian life was like through some of this historical evidence.

Series design: Pardoe Blacker Ltd

First published in 1993 by Wayland (Publishers) Ltd
61 Western Road, Hove, East Sussex BN3 1JD, England

© Copyright 1993 Wayland (Publishers) Ltd

British Library Cataloguing in Publication Data
Gash, Lyn
   Victorian Clothes - (Victorian Life Series)
   I. Title II. Series
   391.00941

ISBN 0 7502 0845 7

Printed and bound in Great Britain by B.P.C.C
Paulton Books Ltd

Cover picture: A woman coming out of widowhood and choosing a dress.

Picture acknowledgements
Barnardos 15; Birmingham Central Library 27; Bridgeman Art Library *cover*, 4; The Butterick Archives, New York 25 (bottom); Cambridge University Library 19 (bottom); Mary Evans Picture Library 9, 10 (both), 11, 20, 21 (top), 23, 24; Hulton-Deutsch Collection 6 (top), 8, 12, 13 (top), 17 (bottom), 25 (top), 26 (both); Illustrated London News 7; Museum of Costume and Fashion Research, Bath 13 (bottom), 14; Norfolk Museums Service (Strangers' Hall Museum) 21 (bottom); Popperfoto 6 (bottom), 16; Poppyland Publishing 19 (top); Punch Picture Library 22; Regimental Museum, Norwich 17 (top); Victoria & Albert Museum 5 (both), 18.

CONTENTS

4

CHANGING WOMEN'S FASHIONS

8

CHANGING MEN'S FASHIONS

12

CHILDREN'S CLOTHES

16

WORKING CLOTHES

20

CLEAN UNDERWEAR

24

BUYING CLOTHES

28 TIMELINE

30 GLOSSARY

31 BOOKS TO READ

32 INDEX

CHANGING
WOMEN'S FASHIONS

When Queen Victoria was crowned in Westminster Abbey in 1837, she wore special clothes to show her importance. New fashionable clothes were an important way of showing your wealth and status in Victorian society. Rich people wore different clothes for different times of the day and always dressed smartly for dinner. They set the fashion for others to copy.

THE SPREAD OF FASHION

The newly married couple in this picture have fine fashionable clothes. Their dress is very different from the clothes of the poor family watching beside the coach.

Even quite poor people could learn what the latest fashions were, by looking at what rich people were wearing. Middle-class people could find out about the latest fashions by reading women's magazines and by looking through new fabrics and fashion pictures in the shops. Everyone wanted to copy the dress styles of the rich.

A newly married couple surrounded by onlookers.

EARLY VICTORIAN STYLES

Tartan was a popular pattern for cloth. Queen Victoria even designed her own tartan and decorated her Scottish castle at Balmoral with it.

The lady in this picture on the left is wearing a tartan dress and her hairstyle is typical of the 1840s. The dress has a long full skirt gathered at a pointed waist. The sleeves join the tight bodice quite low on the arm. It must have been quite difficult for women to raise their arms high or move easily wearing such a costume.

Mrs Maria Jane Wood, 1840s.

LATER VICTORIAN STYLES

Later Victorian dress styles were equally difficult to move in. The full skirt of the 1840s became even fuller in the 1850s and 1860s. Then, by the 1870s the fullness moved to the back of the dress. Look at the way this lady's narrow dress has a lot of material at the back, making a train. Trimmings of bows, frills, lace and extra bands of material were often used to decorate dresses after 1870, especially at the back.

A couple in formal day dress, 1878.

MOURNING CLOTHES

Queen Victoria's husband, Prince Albert, died of typhoid in 1861. From this date, until the end of her life, Queen Victoria dressed in the manner shown in the photograph.

In the past, you were expected to be in 'mourning' after someone in your family had died. 'Mourning' meant black or dull clothes with black crape bands. The closer you were related to the dead person, the longer you wore mourning. Queen Victoria missed her husband so much that she wore black for the rest of her life.

Queen Victoria in 1875.

CLOTHES TO MOVE IN

Life was difficult for women who wanted to be active. In the 1850s women had to run in long skirts, and ride horses keeping both legs together, sidesaddle. Most people felt it was unladylike for women to sweat or do active sports.

After 1880, some ladies' costumes were altered for new popular sports, such as tennis and golf. Sleeves were made less tight and skirts were shortened. Yet the changes were only small. The women in this late Victorian picture on the right are still wearing tight corsets and long skirts for cycling.

Cycling in Hyde Park, about 1900.

THE SEASIDE

If you look at pictures of Victorian seasides, most people are fully clothed. Women carry parasols to protect them from the sun. Browned skin was a sign of being a farm worker and not at all fashionable.

If women did bathe in the sea, they changed in wooden bathing-huts beside the water. The swimsuits were made of thick material that covered most of their legs and bodies. Before the 1870s, many men and boys swam naked. As more women started swimming, men had to wear swimming costumes too.

The beach at St Leonards-on-Sea, 1892.

CHANGING MEN'S FASHIONS

Over the Victorian period, men's clothes became more comfortable. Some clothes that were made for hunting and sport were used as models for a new kind of day wear. Greater attention was paid to the way clothes fitted. England became famous for its tailoring. Compared to women's costume, men's clothes were very plain. They tended to be made of darker and heavier materials and their styles did not change as noticeably as women's.

HOW THE RICH LOOKED SMART

Only the rich could afford to follow fashion closely. They could buy expensive materials and pay tailors and dressmakers to spend a long time adding fine details to their costume. Servants made sure their clothes were always clean and new looking. Poorer people's clothes always looked more crumpled and worn.

The rich man in the right of this picture wears formal day dress, including a standing collar and necktie, underneath a

A rich family at home, 1877.

patterned dressing-gown. Like the two visitors in the picture, all men had to take their hats off indoors. Outdoors, men briefly touched or raised their hats when they met someone they had to show respect to.

A cartoon from *Punch*, 1850.

A MOST ALARMING SWELLING!

EARLY FASHIONS

The artist of the cartoon above is making fun of the 1840s fashion for large cravat bows. Yet these men are fashionable from their heads to their toes. Side whiskers and moustaches were popular throughout the Victorian period. Frock coats were usually left unbuttoned to show off an expensive watch chain and decorative waistcoat. Boldly patterned trousers were often worn in the 1840s and 1850s.

Before the 1800s, men wore knee breeches. By the Victorian period, trousers were usually worn. Only servants, boys and old-fashioned people continued to wear breeches after 1837.

LATER FASHIONS

These smart young men of the 1870s are not so gaily dressed as early Victorians had been. Their jackets are buttoned up: brightly coloured waistcoats are no longer worn. Their ties are smaller and their trousers are plainer.

From the 1860s, men started to wear different styles of jackets. They were not as formal or as long as frock coats. They were sometimes worn with matching trousers and waistcoats. Notice how the men's trousers have no firm crease in them. Creases and turn-ups were not used until the 1890s.

ABOVE: Young men in the 1870s.

A family group wedding photograph from the 1890s.

WEDDING CLOTHES

The bridegroom sits in the centre of the photograph of a middle-class family wedding on page 10. His collar, cuffs and shirt front were separate pieces of heavily starched linen that must have felt like cardboard. They fitted on to his linen shirt with studs. Poorer men had to make do with cotton shirts.

Men would wear the most formal clothes they could afford for their wedding. These included a top hat, a frock coat or a morning coat and a white tie. A bride would often choose a daydress for her wedding day, so this could be worn again. Wedding dresses were not usually white until after the 1870s.

SPORTS CLOTHES

By the end of the Victorian period, rich men had a different style of clothing for each different sport. Some of these clothes also became fashionable casual wear. The comfortable Norfolk jacket was popular country wear after 1850. The homburg hat was made famous by the Prince of Wales, who wore one when out hunting.

Many ordinary people could not afford different costumes for different sports. The people in this picture have adapted their clothes for walking through fields. The woman has tied up her skirt so it does not trail on the ground. The man is wearing leather gaiters to protect his legs.

Partridge-shooting in Norfolk, 1888.

CHILDREN'S CLOTHES

Poor children and rich children were treated very differently. Children from poor families had to go out to work from the age of eleven, or even younger. Their clothes had to be practical and hard-wearing. Rich children did not have to work but they were expected to be quiet and well behaved in front of adults. Their clothes usually copied adult styles and were often uncomfortable to wear.

YOUNG CHILDREN'S CLOTHES

A child in the nursery, 1857.

The child in this picture is a boy. His dress, fancy collar and cotton drawers were typical of Victorian clothes for very young boys.

Boys were 'in petticoats' until they were about five years old. This meant they wore almost identical clothes to girls. Some mothers even kept their sons' hair long, like a girl's. In 1886 a book called *Little Lord Fauntleroy* was published. It encouraged a fashion to dress boys in Little Lord Fauntleroy suits of velvet breeches and jacket, trimmed with a large lace collar.

GIRLS' DRESSES

The middle-class girl in this picture wears a shorter version of her mother's dress. When crinolines or bustles were used by women, girls often wore such things too. Many girls even wore tightly laced corsets so their bodies grew into the necessary fashionable shape.

Girls' skirts would be worn longer as they grew older. At fifteen or sixteen, girls were allowed to join in with the lives of their parents. They put up their hair and wore long dresses.

A girl wearing adult styles, 1876.

A boy in a sailor suit, with his mother.

BOYS' CLOTHES

Victorian boys wore breeches or short trousers with tunics until they were about ten years old. Older middle-class boys wore jackets, waistcoats and stiff collars like their fathers. Working-class boys often wore cut down clothes handed down by fathers and older brothers.

The boy in this photograph wears a sailor suit. Sailor suits for boys became popular after the young Prince of Wales was painted in a sailor outfit in 1846. They were easy to make, cheap to buy and comfortable to wear. By the 1880s, even girls started copying the style for their blouses.

SCHOOL CLOTHES

Ordinary children did not have such fancy clothes as rich children but they still followed the styles of the time. In this photograph, notice the little girl's sailor dress on the left and many of the boys' fancy white 'Little Lord Fauntleroy' collars.

The photograph also shows how young girls protected their dresses with white pinafores. Cotton pinafores were cheaper and easier to wash than dresses. Notice how many of the infants' boots have been mended. Boots were expensive and had to last as long as possible.

POOR CHILDREN

Children from very poor families had to wear ragged second-hand clothes. Yet notice how many of the children below have hats. It was unusual to see Victorian men or boys without a hat outdoors.

Few of the boys have shoes, the most expensive item of clothing. Some country children could not go to school in bad weather because they had no boots or coats to keep them dry and warm.

Poor boys on the street, about 1870.

WORKING CLOTHES

Victorians were fond of uniforms. New kinds of workers such as station masters, postmen and policemen needed new uniforms. Servants had different clothes according to their importance in the household. People who did hard physical work, such as fishermen and farm workers needed practical clothes that let them move easily. They tended to wear old-fashioned clothes, often in a local style.

SERVANTS

Servants did not have to wear special costume unless they worked in the main part of the house. Dark aprons were used for dirty work like cleaning the fires. Some women servants changed into a black dress and white apron for the afternoons when their mistress had visitors.

Housekeeper and servants, 1886.

Very rich families had menservants dressed in 'livery'. This was a brightly coloured uniform in an eighteenth-century style. However, most male servants were dressed more plainly. Horizontal stripes on waistcoats showed that a manservant worked indoors.

SOLDIERS

There were many different soldiers' uniforms. Each regiment had its own styles. Different occasions required changes in uniform – full dress (for parade and when in battle), and informal dress for training and barrack duties. Officers wore more expensive uniforms than ordinary soldiers. Men who were not full-time soldiers were able to wear uniforms by joining part-time volunteer regiments.

Soldiers of the First Batallion, 1870.

After the Crimean War (1853-56), uniforms gradually became more practical and comfortable. From 1885, soldiers in India wore cool khaki uniforms. In the Boer War (1899-1902), when red uniforms were easy targets for the enemy, khaki was first used in battle.

POLICEMEN

Early police uniform was quite like ordinary middle-class dress because the public did not want the police to look like an army. It included a blue frock coat, a blue or white pair of trousers and a reinforced top hat. Only the embroidered letter and number on the stand up collar showed that someone was a policeman.

The uniform was altered in 1864 to a helmet and tunic. The present day truncheon was introduced in 1856 and in 1884 the whistle replaced the policeman's large wooden rattle.

Tom Smith, a London policeman in the 1850s and 60s.

WORKMEN

These porters on the right are wearing thick leather pads over their heads to help them carry heavy loads. The rest of their clothes are typical of working-class dress.

Most working men wore trousers, a waistcoat, a collarless shirt, a jacket and strong boots or clogs. Corduroy, and a cotton and linen fabric called moleskin were popular materials. Most workers preferred a scarf or neckcloth to ties. Caps were seen as a working man's hat by 1900.

COUNTRYMEN AND FISHERMEN

People who lived in isolated places had their own traditions of dress. Countrymen often wore old-fashioned breeches and loose smocks. Fishermen wore waterproof trousers and tunics over knitted jumpers, leg warmers and thick socks. There were local styles of smocking and knitting.

The shape of the sweaters in the picture at the top of page 19 was common to fishermen all over Britain, although the sweater's name 'gansey' originally meant Guernsey. This particular pattern of stitching was typical of the Sheringham area of Norfolk.

Norfolk fishermen.

WOMEN LABOURERS

This picture on the right would have been very shocking to many Victorian people. They thought it was immoral for women to wear men's clothes. Yet in fact trousers were often worn by women labourers. The woman in this picture is wearing trousers which would be lined, and padded at the knee. Many women who worked in mines, brickworks and fishing communities wore trousers because they were safer than skirts. Sometimes, as in this picture, a short skirt or apron was added for the sake of modesty.

Ellen Grounds, a Wigan collier girl, 1873.

CLEAN UNDERWEAR

Red flannel was thought to protect people from illness. Some petticoats and linings were made of it, or a band of red flannel was simply tied around the stomach. Most other underwear was made from white linen or cotton. Corsets, crinolines and bustles were stiffened with whalebone and steel to create the fashionable shape for women. Very little underwear was really comfortable.

A young woman in a corset, 1897.

CORSETS

All Victorian girls wanted waists narrow enough to encircle with their hands. From an early age, they wore tight corsets to train their bodies into the right shape. No wonder Victorian women often fainted!

The woman in this picture is wearing a starched linen corset. The close stitching holds pieces of whalebone or steel in place. A loose shirt is worn under the corset to stop it digging into her skin. She would have needed a servant to lace the corset from behind.

CRINOLINES

The crinoline was invented in the 1850s. This hooped petticoat was so wide that ornaments

and small tables were accidentally knocked over by the person wearing it. In rooms with open fires, it was easy for dresses to catch alight. On windy days, it could blow upwards exposing more underwear. Ladies had to start wearing drawers like young girls to avoid showing their legs. Yet crinolines allowed women to move more freely than the many petticoats worn before. Some women even went mountain climbing in them!

BUSTLES

By about 1870, the crinoline was replaced by the half crinoline or bustle. It allowed for a flatter shape at the front of the dress but supported a mass of dress material gathered in bows and frills at the back. At the same time new sewing and lace machines made decorated underwear cheaper.

The type of bustle shown in this photograph had a spring to allow it to fold up when the wearer was sitting down. By 1890, most women had stopped wearing bustles because the fashion had changed to close-fitting dresses.

Victorian underwear, showing a bustle.

MEN'S UNDERWEAR

This picture shows a washing line of men's underwear. Men's underwear was much simpler than women's. Plain cotton or linen shirts and leggings were usually worn. In the 1870s, writings by Dr Jaeger, a well-known German doctor, were persuading people that wool was more healthy to wear than cotton, especially in winter. Even women started to wear woollen 'combinations', like men. These were an all-in-one suit of drawers and vest, or chemise.

A cartoon from *Punch*, 1876 showing men's underwear.

"O WILD WEST WIND!"

WALKING ABROAD IN ONE OF HIS LOFTIEST MOODS, AND SEEKING FOR INSPIRATION ON A LONELY HEATH, OUR YOUTHFUL POET COMES UPON A LAUNDRY-YARD, AND SEES UNDER-GARMENTS OF ALL SIZES FLAUNTING IN THE GALE.

[Lest the susceptibilities of the more refined should be shocked, we hasten to state that the habiliments depicted above belong exclusively to the Male Sex.

Washing day.

KEEPING CLOTHES CLEAN

Washing clothes was hard work in the Victorian period. Rubbing and wringing had to be done by hand. There were no driers. If it was raining, clothes had to dry indoors. Women had to iron the clothes when they were still damp before they were finally aired. The irons were much heavier than today. Washing, starching and ironing clothes could take over four days. No wonder some families sent their washing out to a laundress!

Poor people did their washing once a week. Middle-class people did it fortnightly. Very rich people had their washing done less often. The more clothes you could afford, the less often you needed to have a wash day.

BUYING CLOTHES

Victorian clothes were not usually bought ready-made. Costumes and underwear were made at home or by a dressmaker. They were made to fit the person exactly. Fabric was expensive and buying material for a garment was a special event. People in the countryside sometimes bought cloth and trimmings from travelling pedlars. People who lived in towns bought from department stores or smaller drapers and haberdashery shops.

SMART DRESS SALONS

These customers are choosing clothes at a well known dress designer's salon. Worth's in Paris and Redfern's in London were particularly famous. Only the very rich could afford to buy their clothes like this. After choosing the style, material and trimmings they liked, customers were measured by shop assistants. They never saw the women who actually made their clothes. The dressmakers worked at the back of the shop, often long into the night, to complete orders in time.

Latest fashions on show, about 1895.

DRESSMAKERS

Most clothes were made by poorly paid dressmakers who worked at home. They visited their customers or received them in their own front parlours. The customer provided the material and design.

The dressmaker in this picture is using one of the sewing machines that started to be used from the mid-1860s. Before then, dresses were made completely by hand.

A dressmaker working at home.

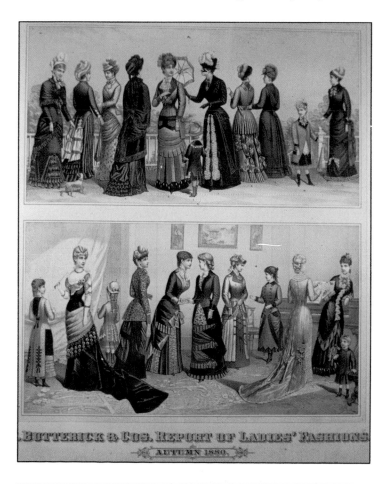

Butterick fashions, 1880.

PAPER PATTERNS

Paper patterns were made for dressmakers in the 1820s. From the 1840s, many Victorian magazines also offered paper patterns for women to make their own clothes. As there were no written instructions or diagrams, some women found them difficult to use. In 1873, the American Butterick Company opened a shop in London. Its cheap patterns for all the family were immediately popular and used widely.

DEPARTMENT STORES

Large department stores, like the one shown in this picture below, sold hats, gloves, shawls, footwear, material and some ready-made clothes. They also had dressmaking departments and workrooms where customers' orders were made up.

Department stores in towns were regarded as the smartest places for making up clothes outside of London. An increasing number of ready-made clothes became available during the Victorian period.

Whiteley's department store, London.

A second-hand clothes shop.

SECOND-HAND CLOTHES SHOPS

Victorians never just threw away old clothes. Rich people would give their out-of-fashion clothes to servants or poorer relations. Quite well-off people altered clothes and hats to keep up with the fashion. Others sold old clothes to dealers or second-hand clothes shops so that they could afford to buy new ones for the next year. Many of the poor relied on these second-hand shops for all their clothes.

Children wearing hand-me-downs.

HAND-ME-DOWNS

Most Victorians had fewer clothes than we have today. One suit for Sunday best and one for weekdays was the standard wardrobe for both men and women.

The eldest children were often the only ones who had clothes specially bought or made for them. Younger children had to make do with clothes that no longer fitted their older brothers or sisters.

The oldest boy in this picture appears to be older than six or seven, the age when most boys started to wear breeches or trousers. He is wearing a dress and pinafore. Perhaps the reason for this is that he is wearing the cast-offs of an older sister.

TIME LINE

	43	410 'THE DARK AGES'	
CELTS	ROMAN BRITAIN	ANGLO-SAXONS	VIKINGS

500

EARLY 1800s

1829 The first police force was set up in London.

1836 Charles Goodyear found a method of treating the surface of gum. This allowed elastic to be used in clothes more easily.

1837 Victoria is crowned Queen in Westminster Abbey.

1840s

1846 The Prince of Wales was painted in a sailor's outfit. The portrait encouraged a fashion among boys for sailor suits.

1849 Walter Hunt invented the modern safety pin.

1850s

Crinolines began to be worn by many women.

1851 Queen Victoria's re-designing of Balmoral Castle in Scotland makes wearing tartan more fashionable.

Isaac Merritt Singer made a sewing machine which became widely used for home and factory dressmaking.

1854-6 Uniforms for soldiers started to become more practical and comfortable.

1860s

1861 Prince Albert died of typhoid.

1864 Policemen's uniforms changed to include a helmet and a tunic.

28

| 1066 | | | | 1485 | 1603 | 1714 | 1837 | 1901 | |

MIDDLE AGES

NORMANS · TUDORS · STUARTS · GEORGIANS · VICTORIANS · 20TH CENTURY

1870s

Fashions encouraged some women to start wearing bustles.

Writings by Dr Jaeger encouraged people to wear more wool, especially for underwear.

1873 The Butterick Paper Pattern Company opened a branch in London.

1880s

Soldiers in India started wearing khaki.

1886 *Little Lord Fauntleroy* by Frances Hodgson Burnett published. The book encouraged a fashion among boys for 'Little Lord Fauntleroy' suits.

1890s

Coat hangers began to be used.

1899-1902 Boer War. Soldiers wore khaki uniforms for the first time in battle.

1900s

1901 Queen Victoria dies.

GLOSSARY

Bodice The upper part of a woman's dress, down to the waist.

Breeches Short trousers fastened below the knee.

Bustle A support worn underneath the back of women's skirts, tied with tapes around a woman's waist.

Chemise Loose shirt or vest, usually worn by women as underwear.

Corset A tight, stiff garment for the body, usually designed to make the waist smaller than normal.

Crape Thin material with a crinkled surface, usually of silk, used for mourning.

Cravat Neckcloth or tie.

Crinoline A hooped petticoat worn under a woman's dress in the 1850s and 1860s.

Drapers A shop that sells cloth and linen.

Drawers Long knickers worn by women ending at the ankle or knee.

Flannel Woven woollen material.

Gaiters Protective leather or canvas coverings for the bottom part of the legs.

Haberdashery Small items of clothing and trimmings.

Homburg hat A hat made of soft felt with a dented crown and stiff upturned brim.

Khaki Dust-coloured cloth, used for army uniform.

Linen Cloth woven from flax, usually used for underwear, shirts and sheets.

Modesty This means not showing off your body. The word can also mean proper behaviour.

Moleskin A hard-wearing cotton and linen fabric used for workclothes.

Norfolk jacket A single-breasted belted jacket with one or two chest pockets and a pleat down the back.

Parasol A sunshade, shaped like an umbrella.

Parlour Sitting room, usually the best room in a Victorian house.

Pedlar An old style of travelling salesman usually selling small items.

Smock A shirt-like garment worn by country labourers.

Status Importance in society.

Tailor Someone who makes made-to-measure clothes, usually for men.

Tunic Loose-fitting shirt or coat, gathered or belted at the waist.

BOOKS TO READ

Brooke, I. *English Children's Costume Since 1775* (A & C Black, 1930)
Herbert, H. *The Clothes They Wore: 19th and 20th Centuries* (Cambridge University Press, 1986)
Hersee, C. & Wainright, C. *Early Victorian Clothes (Clothes from History to Make and Wear)* (Young Library, 1989)

The following are adult books about costume that have been selected for their large number of pictures.
Blum, S. *Victorian Fashions and Costumes from Harper's Bazaar 1867-98* (Dover, 1974)
Buxton, A. *Discovering Nineteenth Century Fashion* (Hobsons, 1989)
Ewing, E. *Everyday Dress 1650-1900* (Batsford, 1984)
Foster, V. *A Visual History of Costume, the Nineteenth Century* (Batsford, 1984)
Ginsburg, M. *Victorian Dress in Photographs* (Batsford, 1982)
Tarrant, N. *Great Grandmother's Clothes, Fashion in the 1880s* (National Museums of Scotland, 1986)
Tozier, J. & Levitt, S. *Fabric of Society, A Century of People and their Clothes 1770-1870* (Laura Ashley, 1983)

PLACES TO VISIT

Many local museums have small collections of costume. It is always worth visiting these to see what they have. Some museums that have large collections include:

ENGLAND

Avon: The Museum of Costume, The Assembly Rooms, Bennett Street, Bath, BA1 2QH. Tel. 0225 461111

Birmingham: City Museum and Art Gallery, Chamberlain Square, Birmingham, B3 3DH. Tel. 021 235 2834

Devon: Devonshire Collection of Costume, Bogan House, High Street, Totnes, TQ9 5RY. Tel. 0803 862423

Paulise de Bush Collection, National Trust Collection of Costume, Killerton House, Broadclyst, Exeter, EX5 3LE. Tel. 0392 881691

Rougemont House, Museum of Costume and Lace, Castle Street, Exeter, EX4 3PU. Tel. 0392 265858

Leicestershire: Wygston's House, Museum of Costume, Applegate, Leicester. Tel. 0533 554100

London: Victoria & Albert Museum, South Kensington, SW7 2RL. Tel. 071 938 8500

Manchester: The Gallery of English Costume, Platt Hall, Rusholme, M14 5LL. Tel. 061 224 5217

Norfolk: Strangers' Hall Museum, 4 Charing Cross, Norwich, NR2 4AL. Tel. 0603 667229

Nottinghamshire: Museum of Costume and Textiles, Castle Gate, Nottingham, NG1 6AF. Tel. 0602 422881

Yorkshire: Castle Howard Costume Galleries, Castle Howard, Malton, York, YO6 7DA. Tel. 0653 84333

SCOTLAND

Dumfries and Galloway: Shambellie House Museum of Costume, New Abbey, Dumfries, DG2 8HG. Tel. 0387 85375

Strathclyde: Paisley Museum and Art Gallery, High Street, Paisley, PA1 2BA. Tel. 041 889 3151

WALES

Glamorgan: Welsh Folk Museum, St Fagan's Castle, Cardiff, CF5 6XB. Tel. 0222 569441

NORTHERN IRELAND

Ulster: Ulster Museum, Botanic Gardens, Belfast, BT9 5AB. Tel. 0232 381251

INDEX

Balmoral, Scotland 5, 28
boots 14, 15, 28
breeches 9, 13, 18, 27
bustle 13, 20, 21, 29

caps 18
combinations 22
corsets 6, 13, 20
countrymen 18
cravat bows 9
crinolines 13, 20, 21, 28

department stores 26
drapers 24
dresses 5, 11, 12, 13, 14, 21, 27
dressmakers 8, 24, 25, 26

fabric/material 24, 25
fishermen 18, 19

hats 9, 11, 15, 17, 26

irons 23

labourers (women) 19
laundress 23

menservants 16
mourning clothes 6

paper patterns 25, 29
pedlars 24
petticoats 21
pinafores 14, 27
policemen 16, 17

safety pin 28
sailor suits 13, 28
school clothes 14
seaside 7
second-hand clothes 15, 26
servants 8, 9, 16, 20
sewing machines 21, 25, 28
soldiers 17, 29
sports clothes 6, 8, 11
swimsuits 7

tartan 5
ties 10, 11, 18
trousers 9, 10, 18, 19, 27

underwear 20-22
uniform 16, 28, 29

waistcoat 9, 10, 13, 16, 18
washing 23
wedding clothes 10-11
workmen 18